Turo MILLIONAIRE SECRETS

Turo MILLIONAIRE SECRETS

Turning Business Credit and Cars Into a Million-Dollar Business

NOELLE RANDALL, MPS, MBA

Copyright © 2022 by Noelle Randall

All rights reserved. In accordance with the U.S. Copyright Act of 1976, the scanning, uploading, and electronic sharing of any part of this book without the permission of the publisher constitute unlawful piracy and theft of the author's intellectual property. If you would like to use material from the book (other than for review purposes), prior written permission must be obtained by contacting the publisher at books@waltonpublishinghouse.com Reviewers may quote brief passages in reviews.

Walton Publishing House
Houston, Texas
www.waltonpublishinghouse.com
Printed in the United States of America

The advice found within may not be suitable for every individual. This work is purchased with the understanding that neither the author nor the publisher is held responsible for any results. Neither author nor publisher assumes responsibility for errors, omissions, or contrary interpretations of the subject matter herein. Any perceived disparagement of an individual or organization is a misinterpretation.

Brand and product names mentioned are trademarks that belong solely to their respective owners. Library of Congress Cataloging-in-Publication Data under

ISBN: 978-1-953993-48-9 Paperback)
ISBN: 978-1-953993-47-2 (Digital/ E-book)

Disclaimer: All documents in this book are intended for the use of the reader as a sample to edit only and not to copy. These documents remain the property of Noelle Randall Coaching and thus may be confidential and/or legally privileged or otherwise protected.

The success of our students is the only reason we exist, they come first in everything we do. We are strong advocates of learning, doing, and teaching to create lasting improvements in our community.

Dedication

I dedicate this book to my brother, who is passionate about cars and has inspired me to expand my business and take it to the next level! You have given me so much knowledge about the car industry, and I am grateful.

To the intelligent person who picked this book up, I am proud of you for taking the initiative of starting your entrepreneurial journey today.

Thank you!

CONTENTS

Introduction 11

Chapter I: Turo: The Real Deal 13
Chapter II: Business Strategy: Pick Your Niche 23
Chapter III: Setting up Your Turo Account 43
Chapter IV: Renting Your Vehicle 59
Chapter V: Check-in and Check-out Process 71
Chapter VI: Protecting Your Vehicle 81
Chapter VII: Car Acquisition and Financing 87
Chapter VIII: Lead Explosion: Marketing 93
Chapter IX: Diversify Your Portfolio 101
Chapter X: Credit Repair 105
Chapter XI: Build a Successful Business 117

About Noelle 123
Connect with Noelle 125

Introduction

The economy is changing quickly, and now more than ever, you need to have a plan to build generational wealth. I love how entrepreneurs are becoming more innovative, and companies are setting up structures where everyday people can win and win big! That is how I felt when I discovered the world of Turo. I hope that as you read the pages of this book, you will be inspired to do something new.

This is my fifth book for future and current entrepreneurs highlighting additional ways to create wealth. I will continue to offer you the knowledge that puts you on the wealth path. It is on this path that I have made millions of dollars and have helped hundreds of thousands of people just like you do the same.

You may already know my story. In a nutshell, I started from the bottom in real estate, expanded into coaching others, and started fulfilling my life's purpose. I challenged myself to keep growing, constantly stretching myself to become a better me. I was not lucky. I did not become a millionaire accidentally. My success is not because I rubbed a genie in a bottle. I reached my success because

I kept going- even on the days I did not feel like it. People often tell me they love my energy. I love hearing that because it tells me others can feel my passion for seeing them win.

As we continue on another learning path, I want you to take notes and quickly take action. Money is attracted to speed and implementation, and the sooner you get started, the sooner you can see your profit hitting your bank account. **So, step into the winner's circle as I teach you another way to help you achieve your dreams.**

To Your Success!

Noelle

CHAPTER I

TURO: THE REAL DEAL

> "*Innovation is taking two things that already exist and putting them together in a new way.*"
> Tom Freston

What if I told you that you could flip your personal vehicle into a cash cow? How would you feel about turning that car sitting in your driveway into a six and seven-figure business? Trust me. I am not exaggerating. With the Turo car-sharing platform we'll be discussing throughout this book, you can set yourself up for an abundance of success and wealth if you are willing to do the work necessary. It has always been my goal to bring you new ways to create millions in business, and this is another fantastic platform I have studied and mastered to bring you the actual "how-to" of attaining success.

I was so committed to learning how to master Turo and turn it into a money-making machine that I spent months researching and learning how the process works. I never thought something like this would exist in the marketplace. But when you think about it, why wouldn't consumers catch on to a concept like this? Most people, when traveling, will need to rent a car. Some people even need to rent cars locally as well. A car in most parts of the world is a necessity. Because of this, this vehicle of making money will be an ever-growing platform. Before Turo, the major car rental companies dominated the market. The car rental market accounted for $86 billion in 2020 and is expected to reach $131 billion by 2026. As of 2020, Turo reported 14 million members and 450,000 operating vehicles across 56 countries." They offer over 850 unique makes and models available in the United States, Canada, the United Kingdom, and abroad. With the Turo platform, you will have an opportunity to enjoy a slice of this pie.

How Turo Works

As we start this book together, this section will give you a general overview of how Turo works. It is relatively easy to understand, especially if you are knowledgeable about the Airbnb model. Turo, like Airbnb, is a peer-to-peer sharing platform where you can list your cars for rent and compete in a global marketplace. I love my Airbnb business and coming across the Turo advertisement caught my attention. I am quite familiar with Airbnb, with many of my rentals listed on the platform. It has been a consistent stream of income in my business. My last book, "BNB Millionaire Secrets, The Real Blueprint to Short Term Rental," is written about the platform. But honestly, cars were never a business model I thought about for myself, and I never considered turning them into a business.

Before researching this platform, I considered cars a depreciating asset, but after digging deeper and discovering that Turo was indeed the Airbnb for cars, I had a mindset shift. I became interested in purchasing and leasing cars as business assets. The platform offered anyone with a decently maintained vehicle to make money. With Turo, it doesn't matter if you have an economy car like a Honda Civic or an exotic car like a Lamborghini Gallardo; you can list your car and get paid daily for sharing it with traveling guests.

After a bit more due diligence, I checked if it was available in my city and how easy it would be for me to sign up and list my cars. Once I felt comfortable, I downloaded the app and decided to test it out. I was impressed with my first initial contact. The app was seamless with in-app messaging, making it easy and convenient for hosts and guests to communicate. There were plenty of pictures of the vehicle I was interested in with the ability for me to assess everything I needed about the rental. It was just like Airbnb, even the check-in and check-out process. I rented a luxury car for a couple of days for the complete experience. It was super easy, user-friendly, and efficient. I was impressed with the state of the Range Rover I picked up. The host kept the car cleaned and maintained without too many miles. It truly exceeded my expectations.

After having such a good rental, I quickly researched how to convert Turo into a business model. As entrepreneurs, we should always look for ways to identify additional income streams that require little time usage. In other words, we should actively seek more passive income opportunities. In my preparation and research, I began to ask questions from those I knew who were car enthusiasts because they could tell me all about the cars that would work well and handle wear and tear. They also advised me which cars to avoid without having to break the bank to purchase them or have expensive upkeep. I wanted reliable cars with good gas fueling. The car's safety was important, as well as how easy and cost-efficient the maintenance would be.

Savvy entrepreneurs count the cost before starting any new venture. I have learned an essential skill in business: to ask and learn from the experts, so it will make things easier and ultimately save me money. Many people get stuck on the capital they need to start the business, but I knew more than capital was needed to succeed in this business. You must also acquire suitable cars to help make day-to-day operations more manageable and profitable. For me, purchasing and financing my cars made sense to grow and scale quickly. The beauty of Turo is that you do not need to own your car or have the capital to be successful. I will be sharing more about this.

Start With Turo Today!

I'm sure you will not need much convincing after reading this book, but like anyone starting this business, you may be skeptical about using your personal vehicle to rent out. It makes perfect sense to be concerned about your vehicle's wear and tear or potential damage. With any business, there is a form of liability you take on. I do not want to paint the picture that there will be no hiccups. But I want to help alleviate your stress about the idea. Renting with Turo is safe. In fact, the company has an option for protection plans for owners. Outside of your personal and commercial auto policy, the extra tier of protection can help cover the cost of a rental car while yours is being repaired. It also covers lost rental income from your car's downtime.

Like any other business, it is up to you to do your due diligence. Visit their website at www.turo.com and review their policies, terms, and conditions to ensure it is a good fit. A good idea for one person may not be suitable for you. Nevertheless, I highly recommend the platform, which is why I wrote this book.

The Business Behind Turo

You may be wondering how you can make money with Turo. With Turo, you can start with just one car and grow it into a fleet of cars, as my company has done, and it is what we teach our students to do. Not only can you rent your cars for a daily and nightly rate, but you can also rent luxury and exotic cars for video shoots, photoshoots, and business events. The money you can make with Turo is endless. This may sound too good to be true, but it is not. Throughout this book, you will learn about Turo, how to use it to make a lot of money, and things you should do to make the most money possible with your account. In addition, I will be sharing with you everything you need to know about the car rental platform.

The way that Turo works is if you are a host (the person putting their car up for rent), you can list your car, and once it is booked, Turo receives a fee out of your booking costs, and you receive the rest. The more your car is rented, the more you make. With Turo's active platform, new potential customers are enrolling daily. If you position your car correctly, add a description that stands out, and price your car for profit, you will make good money. I make anywhere from $500- $1,500 per month per vehicle in profit. Yes, you read that correctly. This is what we are currently averaging with a fleet of over 13 cars. This platform has been a game-changer.

Here is just a small example to get your mind going on how this process works. I have a 2021 Range Rover that rents for $299 a day on Turo, plus gas fees, car washes, and extras. If this car rents for ten days, I can make close to $3,000 monthly. And even with my car note, I make a substantial profit.

You may not own a high-end car like a 2021 Range Rover, and that is perfectly alright. I also own a 2019 Nissan Altima that gets rented out for about $40 daily. Again, even renting this out for 10-12 days, I make my car note with some extra. You do not always have to have the most expensive cars to make a profit. You can do it with the more practical cars, like Nissans, Hondas, Hyundais.

One of the top 10 cars currently renting on the platform is a Prius, which shows how profitable the business can be with the right mindset and process to set up your business. So, you can get out there and make as much money as you want.

Are There Cons?

There is no perfect business, and I always believe in being transparent about what to expect. I've received this question quite a bit, and it makes sense to know all sides of the business. Although there is lots of money to be made, with anything, there are pros and cons. So before diving in too deep, let's address the not-so-good side of renting cars.

Con #1- Depreciation

The first major downside is cars are considered depreciating assets. This means after a while; they lose value the more miles they are driven. If you own a vehicle for three to four years and decide to sell it, you will most likely have to sell it for much less than what you paid. "After one year, your car will probably be worth about 20% less than what you bought it. After that steep first-year dip, that new car will depreciate by 15–25% yearly until it hits the five-year mark. So, after five years, that new car will lose around 60% of its value."

Con #2- High Mileage

Another con is having so many miles on your cars. On a typical month, I can have ten rentals. Each trip can add up to a thousand miles over the weeks and months. Before long, the mileage adds up quickly, accumulating thousands and thousands of miles on my car. So, you may wonder what happens after these cars reach high miles. Well, there are a few options I put into place for that. When I purchase my cars, they are generally new or used with no more than 20,000- 30,000 miles. I monitor the mileage on the cars and trade them in after they hit 100,000. I maintain higher rental limit options on my economy and mid-range cars when renting my cars. This is not the situation with my high-end cars, where I have limited miles. Although I can control the mileage a bit, the reality is there are still lots of mileage being driven each month.

Con #3- Car Damage

Cars are easy to damage in a car accident. As the car owner and host, you should have a reserve for repairs and minor tune-ups. Turo has policies in place, and if there are not any scratches or dents, once they're over a specific size, they will cover the damage with their insurance coverage. Be sure to read Turo's policy on car damage and reimbursement policy.

Con#4 - Vehicle Theft

Another good point to discuss is car theft. You may be wondering, what if my car is stolen? Yes, I get it. You may have heard horror stories about cars being stolen. It is true; cars can be stolen, just like the everyday car you drive. But honestly, I have never had that experience. As a good business owner, I put things in place like trackers on my cars. In fact, I have two trackers on each of my cars. Teslas and Jeeps are great cars that are equipped with devices. So, I know where those vehicles are always. I know when they start or stop. Some cities have higher risks for theft than others, so do your research. For example, you can check for cars more prone to theft. I cannot stress it enough that you must do your homework.

I hope this chapter gave you a good overview of Turo. We will be digging deeper as you keep reading but now is an excellent time to assess if this is a business you can see yourself operating. Knowing the pros and cons of the business, are you still interested in moving forward? If so, let's keep going.

> *Visit Crfortunes.com to get access to my course that will teach you more secrets on car rentals. Use code "Noelle 40" for huge savings!*

CHAPTER II

BUSINESS STRATEGY: PICK YOUR NICHE

"If Opportunity Doesn't Knock, Build a Door."
Milton Berle

If you are still reading, it is safe to assume you have accepted both the pros and cons of the Turo business, and you are ready to test the water. That is great news. Let's go ahead and address first things first. Before starting your Turo business, ensure your business entities are set up correctly, whether you have a few cars or an entire fleet. I discussed how to set up your business extensively in "Millionaire Business Secrets, The Real Beginners Guide to Starting a Business," if you have not set up your business yet, refer to that guide.

The Right Mindset

Personal development and the right mindset are the foundational tools needed to succeed in any venture. Before you become too invested in planning your business do a self-check to make sure you are mentally prepared for this journey. You can have all the knowledge in the world, but if you do not have the "wealthy mindset," you will never attract the millions waiting on you. It starts with your mindset if you want to increase your current income and have more freedom. There are no shortcuts to this; you should not ignore this principle. You must be willing to change and elevate your mindset to become better. Being successful is not just how much money you have in your bank account or how much money you can potentially earn. It starts with your mindset. You must be able to visualize your success before you see the manifestation of your success.

Also, be careful of your environment because if you are surrounded by negativity, it will affect the growth. If you are in an environment that does not support a healthy and wealthy mindset, it is time for you to change your circle. You must be willing to let go of those who do not feed your flame or do not support your goals. Every

BUSINESS STRATEGY: PICK YOUR NICHE

successful person has had to do this. Not that you do not love these people or have a good relationship with them; having them around negatively affects your business. You cannot afford to be surrounded by negative people; you are just going to become as damaging as they are. It is not unusual in business to have those self-doubts. To free yourself from this, you must shift the things you hear, see, and are connected to.

If you want to become a millionaire, you need to surround yourself with those who make more money or are more financially established than you. Surround yourself with those who boost you and push you to be better than you are. If you want to become a millionaire, you must start hanging around with millionaires. Interestingly, they are more prevalent than you think. So, if you are planning to leave your 9 to 5, you have to start hanging around more entrepreneurs and start getting around more people who are more optimistic.

Success in business starts with a vision; make sure you sit down and think about your business. Think about what problem you want to solve and what your business will be. Be honest and realistic with what you can manage. Also, be careful when you are starting your business that you do not overextend yourself by putting your hands in everything.

Getting Started

#1- Pick Your Niche and Identify Your Ideal Customer

Knowing *who* you serve is a key to your business success, as I mentioned earlier. This is also known as your niche or your specialty. Within your Turo business niche, you want to choose a specific problem you will be solving, i.e., whether you deal in economy cars, luxury cars, or exotic cars. You want to start your business by dealing with one problem that you will be solving.

You must know who your ideal customer/ guest will be. Knowing this will help you determine the types of cars you purchase and the options you incorporate into your fleet. Are you looking to attract guests that are more budget-focused? If so, an economy fleet of cars will be good for you. Are you looking to attract wealthy or business professionals? If so, a luxury fleet of cars is where you should aim. Being specific upfront will save you a lot of heartaches, even when it comes down to marketing your business. Knowing what your guest/ renter values will aid you in offering attractive features and extras that keep them renting with you. This leads to great reviews for you as a host.

#2 Determine Your Business Model

After you've picked your niche and identified your ideal customer, you will need to determine the business model that works best for you. There are four ways you can get started with your car rental business. You can be an owner, have a joint venture, use leveraging, or you can be a broker. Let's go a bit deeper into each of these below.

Owner

Being an owner simply means that you use your own money, credit, etc., for your business. Everything starts and ends with you. As an owner, you inherit all the risks of your business, but you also keep the total profits made. As an owner, you take on the responsibility to grow your business, plan everything out, create the procedures, and create the steps and find the cars all of this.

Owners are generally self-funded, which means they use their own money. This may seem as if it is hard to do, but it is really not. Typically, owners can implement various avenues to fund their business. For example, they can leverage their 401k or take out personal loans for their business startup capital. Business credit is another option for self-funding. I will be going further into how to get approved for business credit in chapter 9.

It is said that everything rises and falls on the owner. Do not look at being an owner as a negative if you have to begin your journey doing it by yourself. If you have the money or business credit, you can quickly get started without needing anyone to co-sign or limit how quickly you can grow your business. I remember speaking with one of my coaches at Noelle Randall Coaching about this very thing. KJ Steir mentioned when he started, there were people who talked about starting and helping him, but they were not as serious and willing to get started with him. They wanted to see him do it first, and that is not unusual. Sometimes people may want to see others do it first before they are willing to invest any money or give help because they may not see the vision or they are not willing to take the risk. That often happens with new business ventures. But when no one else is willing to help you, do not let that discourage you. You put some skin in the game and keep focused until you see the wins. You must be willing to believe in yourself and go out there and do it yourself. One of the bright sides of being an owner is you get to reap all the rewards by yourself.

There are perks to being an owner. You have the freedom to choose without having someone looking over your shoulder or adding resistance if they do not like your suggestions. As an owner, you get to make business decisions without any resistance. When shopping for a car, you get to choose the car you want. You can get the color you want and any of the features that you would want your guests to have.

Joint Venture

Another type of business model is the joint venture model. This is where you have a business partner or multiple partners. In a joint venture, an agreement is made with the breakdown of how the business will operate. There is generally a partner that runs the company and another partner that provides the capital and is a silent investor. With this, they use their credit and/ or money to purchase the fleet needed to get the business fully operational.

Joint ventures are one of the easiest ways to get into this business, especially if you know people with capital or know someone that wants to partner with you. Business can be a lot of work, so if you can find someone to provide capital while you provide the sweat equity or vice versa, consider it. You can partner to do it together instead of doing it all by yourself.

Leveraging

You can also get started in your Turo business by leveraging. This is when you're either using your credit or someone else's credit to finance the fleet of cars for your business. Leveraging is not only credit, but it can also be social currency. In the world we live in today, social media influencers are the drivers behind many successful brands. The influence they have to get others to want to buy is also identified as currency. Social currency is the status that you have in society, whether you are an influencer, a movie star, a famous person, or a wealthy person. Social currency is the power you unknowingly get once you become popular within society.

This can help influence people to lend you cars because they trust you because of who you are. You may also have social currency with your friends because they trust you based on who you are and what you've done. They may be willing to assist you in any way they can.

Brokering

Lastly, let's discuss brokering. Brokering between two people is a brilliant way to create a win-win for all parties. An example of brokering in the Turo business is when you have potential guests/renters but do not have enough cars to rent to them, so you utilize someone else's vehicles for your customers, with their permission, of course. The beauty of brokering is that you do not need to own cars. This can be a friend's car or another business owner's car. You can broker with other hosts or those who have fleets and use their vehicles to satisfy your customers' needs. With brokering, you use your social currency to leverage the agreement. An important component of brokering is making sure the person you are brokering the deal with is earning money in exchange.

An Example of Brokering

Let's say you have ten potential guests, but you do not have any cars to rent. Your friend John down the street has ten exotic cars that he is looking to rent out but doesn't have a customer base. You both need what the other person has.

John wants to earn $10,000 per month, but he is not making this because his fleet is sitting and not being rented out.

You want to earn $4,000 per month, but you do not have the vehicles that will generate the cash flow you want.

You and John would enter a brokering deal to help you both reach your goals. In this brokering agreement, you would structure a deal with John that helps him makes the profit that he wants. If $10,000 per car is his goal, put an agreement detailing the amount you will pay him. Another perk to brokering is that John really is not concerned about what you are charging the guests to rent, although I always suggest you be upfront about what you are charging. Most owners will not mind if they receive the amount you both agreed to. Anything that you earn over this amount is profit.

I absolutely love brokering deals, and when done correctly, you can earn money without the expensive overhead. It benefits both parties. A deal is when everybody wins, and that is what you want when you are a broker in these deals. You want to put everybody in the position to win. You are getting more cars to add to your fleet, and you make your business partner or this person you are doing business with, they are making the money they want. It is an amazing feeling when both parties are linked up, and they get what they want. And, after six months, if everything is going great, you can renegotiate or keep the same deal and do it again for as long as you want. You can instead do it for another six months or a full year's contract.

When you first begin brokering deals, I highly recommend you start with a six-month contract to assess whether or not the deal is a good fit. If things work out well, you will have an opportunity to renegotiate after six months. A successful brokering relationship requires trust and integrity. Be a person that keeps your word and is careful not to damage the relationship. This goes back to social currency. If owners are willing to allow you to rent their vehicles, they obviously trust you. Do not jeopardize that. Another perk to brokering is it is a great way to network as well, and you can learn how to partner up with other owners who have fleets using their cars at no real liability to yourself. This is how you make a ton of money without having to extend yourself.

At the end of this chapter, I have included a sample agreement. As always, have your attorney review any agreement used.

Another Example of How a Brokered Deal Works

Jim and Tracey decide to enter into a partnership. Jim has multiple exotics cars. He has a couple of Rolls Royce's, but he does not have the customer base to occupy those cars, and they are sitting in his garage, not making him any money. Tracey has access to customers, but she does not have a fleet of exotic cars, and her client base will be willing to rent them out. They both need something the other has and decide to enter into a brokering agreement. It ultimately is a win-win for both parties.

As part of their agreement, Tracey will take on the responsibility of finding renters for the vehicles. She will also market the vehicles with her fleet of economy mid-range cars (if she owns any). To make this deal work, Tracey should find out how much Jim wants to profit from his cars each month. Ideally, she will make a deal where she offers Jim the minimum that he is willing to charge for the vehicles, plus she will add her fees on top of that in order to make a profit. If Tracey's arrangement is to pay Jim $1,500 per month, she becomes obligated to pay that amount. No matter what, she must make sure he gets his portion of the money.

In your agreement, you would state everything you are responsible for. At the bare minimum, it will be your responsibility to maintain the car and ensure it is drivable and does not have car damage. If the car is involved in an accident while under your care, you would have to cover it or make sure you have the funds or the means to repair the car.

How You Make Money in a Brokered Deal

In the above scenario, Jim's cost to use his vehicle is $1,500, but what about Tracey? How does she make money? Tracey should charge her fee on top of his base amount. Starting from the base of Jim's $1500, she can charge an additional $700 over this amount and charge the renter $2,200 per month. She can charge even more to make more profit per month.

Calculating Profit

If her responsibility is to pay $1,500 to Jim every month, she will divide that amount by 30 to get the daily cost, which would be $50. Knowing that exotic cars rent for triple that amount, she can charge up to $150 per day. Once she pays Jim his agreed amount of $1,500, she will keep the $3,000 profit.

That is the biggest benefit of brokering cars because you have the clientele who want the cars. Your partner, the person you are going to be brokering with, only has the vehicle with no means to create a cash flow, and so this is why it is a great option for you to broker deals with people who have nice cars and have no way to actually make money on them. This works well with luxury and exotic cars.

Let's do a quick recap. In your personal agreement, the bare minimum is that:

- You will be responsible for taking care of the car.
- Ensuring it is drivable
- In case of an accident, you will cover the repair.

These are your liabilities. Your responsibility is to make the payment per your agreement. The benefit of brokering cars is the ability to make a profit off the clientele that you know, creating a win-win for both parties.

The Downside to Brokering

There aren't many downsides to brokering deals because you are making a clear arrangement that details expectations to limit the downsides. However, since we know any business, even a good model like brokering does have some areas that must be considered before deciding if this model works for you.

The biggest downside to brokering is the added responsibilities that come with maintaining and creating the revenue that your business partner wants. With any joint venture, you have to be able to answer these questions.

- Can you trust the person?
- Can they trust you?
- Can you secure the money you said you would in the agreement?

Also, keep in mind if the original terms do not work, you can assess and renegotiate the terms. Maybe after brokering for six months, you decide you no longer want to be responsible for the car's maintenance cost. This can all be negotiated to limit any downside to the arrangement. It can be similar to any joint venture, so make sure your agreement fully includes what you need in order to make the partnership successful for both parties involved.

#3 Create a Plan for Success

After you have picked a niche and decided on your business model, planning for your success is next. You must have a solid plan for growth and success in your business. Your plan should include

BUSINESS STRATEGY: PICK YOUR NICHE

your income goals, your marketing research and strategy, and your daily execution plan. Run your Turo business like any other business. This is not a get-rich-quick venture, so do not expect it to be an overnight process. It can be a fun process, and by fun, I mean you get to be creative with how you want your business to operate without any limits or restrictions, but it still will require your efforts.

Do not rush the process of success. Think about who you are, what your business stands for, what problem you are going to be solving, and how you can solve that problem. Think about who you are serving and what your operational hours will be. Think about where you are today and plan from there. Be organized and deliberate in your business. Organize the entire business from start to finish. Planning is half the battle, and when you are organized, things move much smoother and much easier for you.

The achievements of your business are in your hands, and not anybody else's- it is up to you. You hold the key to reaching your millions. Your success, your business, and earning the money you want to acquire all depend on you. You must have the willpower and drive to push yourself to get what you want in life. If you want your business to excel, you must internalize that you will be successful. The way for this to manifest into fruition is for you to push yourself and have that 'Go-Getter Attitude.'

Lastly, I'd like to encourage you to set your expectations correctly. I understand you want to be successful as quickly as possible; however, do not rush into success. This is why wealthy people stay wealthy because they do not run. They set an expectation for when they're going to reach their success. Give yourself time.

Your business may not explode the second you get in because it requires grit and persistence. If you leap too quickly without the proper preparation, you can end up burning yourself out, and your business will never flourish to its potential. Give yourself time. It may take a year or two for you to reach your business goals. Be patient with your process. Every successful person started from somewhere. Continue to work towards your millionaire status, and you'll get there with the right planning and execution.

Top Ten Rented Cars

Best Types of Cars to List

Toyota Corolla
Ford Mustang
Toyota Camry
Jeep Wrangler
BMW 3 Series
Tesla Model 3
Honda Civic
Hyundai Elantra
Mercedes Benz C-Class

Bonus Cars

Jeep Grand Cherokee
Tesla Model X
Chevy Camaro
Audi A3[1]

---

[1] James McCandless, "10 Most Popular Cars Turo Renters Choose," News Week, 11/3/21, https://www.newsweek.com/10-most-popular-cars-renters-choose-turo-1644135, (accessed February 15th 2022)

Vehicle Use Agreement Guideline (SAMPLE)

Definitions: The "Owner" is the person who has legal ownership of the vehicle. The "User" is the person who has right of temporary use of the vehicle for the specified period. The "Owner's Agent" is the person designated to act on behalf of the owner.

We, the undersigned, agree to the following conditions. This agreement is between _____, herein called "Owner," and herein called "User."

1. DESIGNATED VEHICLE INFORMATION

Make _____
Model _____
VIN _____
Color _____
Year _____
Tag _____
Mileage_____

2. TERM

The dates for use of the vehicle will be: from _____ to_____ (DD/MM/YYYY).

3. INSURANCE

The Owner is to provide the User with the registration papers and a copy of the insurance policy for the borrowed vehicle. The Owner, or Owner's Agent, will pay all insurance and registration fees in host country.

The User will pay all personal insurance fees and provide proof of current driver's insurance. In addition, the User is to provide a letter to the Owner's insurance company to verify his/her safe-driving record and proof of personal insurance.

4. CONDITION OF CAR

The Owner will ensure that the vehicle is clean and in good mechanical condition. All major systems should be recently checked (steering, brakes, electrical components, ignition, cooling, transmission, suspension, motor and tires) and "Certificate of Mechanical Fitness" obtained. The motor should be tuned and serviced. The replacement of oil and air filters should be carried out just prior to the start date in this agreement.

The Owner should provide the User with a list of any minor defects in the vehicle.

5. MAINTENANCE AND REPAIR

A. Routine Maintenance
1. The vehicle is to be serviced according to the service manual provided. (Or as instructed by the Owner.)

2. The User is responsible for all basic service costs.

B. Breakdowns and Repairs

1. The Owner is responsible for any costs that can be attributed to mechanical failure due to normal usage for which the vehicle was designed.

2. The User is to contact the Owner or the Owner's Agent if such a mechanical failure should occur to obtain authorization to have repairs carried out quickly. Accounts are to be presented to the Owner or the Owner's Agent for payment.

3. The User is responsible for any costs incurred that can be attributed to neglect or misuse of the vehicle.

C. Accidents and Repairs

1. The conditions of the insurance policy for the vehicle is to be complied with if accidents, theft, and damage associated with theft occur.

2. The User is responsible for the basic excess on the policy.

3. Repair costs, if less than $500, are to be paid by the User.

4. Accidents are to be reported to the police within 24 hours if damage has occurred or a person has been injured.

5. Any increased premium rates placed on the policy are to be paid by the User for two years.

6. In the case of an accident for which the User is not at fault, claims will be made on the other party's insurance at no cost to the Owner of the vehicle.

7. If the Owner's Insurer refuses to meet a claim as a result of any action by the User allowing the Insurer to void the claim (e.g., drink driving, invalid license, negligence) then the User shall be responsible for the claim, or claims, in its, or their, entirety.

D. Cleaning and Sanitizing

1. The User is responsible for registering the Vehicle with the Car Washing Service and responsible for maintaining the account and keep it in good standing until the end of the agreed term of use of the vehicle.

6. USE

The vehicle is to be driven on properly constructed road surfaces in good condition or on leveled-off road surfaces only.

The vehicle shall be listed on Peer-to-Peer car sharing platforms with all proceeds being paid directly to the User.

7. LICENSE/LAW

All designated drivers will obtain the appropriate license for that country and will comply with the relevant laws concerning motor vehicle use in that country.

8. FEES

The User is responsible for all fees and fines (including, but not limited to, speeding tickets, parking tickets, etc.) relating to use of vehicle.

The User shall be paid $350/month or 20% of profits, whichever is higher, for managing the Owner's vehicle that is listed on any or all Peer-to-Peer Car sharing platforms.

9. MILEAGE

The vehicle may be driven: An unlimited distance

-OR-

Shall not be driven a distance of more than _____

10. REPORTING

The User will provide the following reports to the Owner as proof of reported income of the Vehicle

- Monthly Income Report
- Gas Receipts/Report
- Misc. Items

11. OTHER POINTS MUTUALLY AGREED UPON

Owner's Name _____

Owner's Signature _____

Date _____

User's Name _____

User's Signature _____

Date _____

Effective Date _____ Ending Date _____

CHAPTER III

SETTING UP YOUR TURO ACCOUNT

> *"Innovation distinguishes between a leader and a follower."*
> Steve Jobs

In this chapter, we'll discuss how to set up your Turo account. With every new account, there is an approval process for Turo. You can usually expect verification to take at least 24-48 hours to verify your account. Before setting up your account, research to ensure your vehicle meets Turo's list of universal requirements. You can find more about this on Turo's website. Below is a sample list of what you will need:[2]

- Be registered in any state except New York
- Vehicle no more than 12 years old
- Carry personal or commercial insurance
- Have fewer than 130,000 miles
- Have a clean (e.g. not a "branded" or "salvage") title
- Have never been declared a total loss

Setting up a new account is relatively easy. You will need your license plate number and photos of your car, driver's license, and contact information. In addition, you'll need to provide the following:

1. **Your Location:**

The first question in the account setup is, "where is your car located." You must provide a physical address for your account

2. **VIN#:**

---

[2] "Meeting vehicle requirements | US," Turo, https://help.turo.com/en_us/vehicles-we-accept-rylmrNl45#article-title-2, (accessed January 6th, 2022)

Your VIN # is needed next, so have that handy. You want to pay attention to the little box below it: My model year is 1981 or later. Be sure to answer this correctly.

3. **Mileage:**

From the VIN, you will need to have your mileage. Any car over 140k miles will not be accepted.

4. **Automatic or Manual:**

From there, choose if the vehicle is automatic or manual. This is very important, so make sure you're choosing the right one. There are

5. **Financial Goals:**

From there, it'll ask you about your goals for the car.

What is your primary financial goal for the car?

Other questions include:

How often do you use the vehicle?

How often do you want to share your vehicle? If this is your business, I always select "often" and not "always."

Your goals for the car

Car availability. (As a side note for this question choose six to twelve hours advance notice.

You can set the maximum trip line from one day to three months. I suggest you make your maximum bookings in two-week increments. If the renter needs to extend, they will have to request the car.

6. Vehicle Description:

When you reach this section, input your license plate number, the state the vehicle is in, and your vehicle features. I suggest you put as many features as. The website will give you the option of using 100 words; I usually use 250. Adding more to your descriptions will help you get the best listings possible. Renters will read the details, so you want to stand out from the competitors as much as possible.

In the description, list things like:

- The number of seats in your car.
- The number of doors on your car.
- Cleanliness expectations.
- Whether it is a pet-friendly car.
- Whether your mileage limit is flexible.

Before listing your car, view the descriptions from various superhosts and pay attention to how they listed their vehicles. Notice the details they use for their listing. Look at what they are saying about the car model you are listing as well as other similar make and models. If you are listing a BMW I8, look out for people who have a BMW I8 regardless of the year. You do not have to re-create the wheel. You want to be competitive with the other hosts in your area, and the way to do that is to see what they are listing about their cars and enhance your listing. To be a successful entrepreneur, you must creatively look at what other successful entrepreneurs are doing and improve it. At the end of this chapter, are some listings examples you can use as a template to create your listing. Feel free to alter the text to suit the listing for your car.

7. Photos

The more appealing your car photos can make a difference in the number of bookings you receive. Not having clear and quality photos lessen your chances of your vehicle being booked on a consistent basis, so make sure you spend time planning your photos. You can opt to have these professionally taken by a photographer, or you can take the photos yourself. If you are going to do it for yourself, there are a couple of things you should know so you can take good pictures. It is essential that you have a good camera. Whether it is an actual camera or you have a good camera on your phone, whatever you choose to use, make sure it is quality. I recommend you research how to take the best photos and angles of your vehicle on YouTube. Research tips and tricks for the best images, angles, and scenery. Please do not just walk outside with your smartphone and take snapshots without proper planning. You want your listing to be professional, so do not skimp on the quality photos of your vehicles.

If you decide to hire a professional, here are a couple of things I highly recommend you ask the photographer so you are not wasting their time or your money. First, ask them if they have ever had a photo shoot for a car before. Not every photographer has done this type of work, and there could be a difference between the photography services they offer and what you are asking them to do. If they have experience with photoshoots for cars, request to check some of their work. Ask them for referrals of their past clients. You are fully obligated to do your due diligence when you hire a professional to do any work for you. Another question to ask your photographer is if they can edit your photo. If not, you can edit the images if you know how to edit photos professionally, or you can hire a freelancer via Upwork or Fiverr. Let me offer this as a bonus. If you have the budget or your photographer has access to a drone, use it. You can take photos with a drone and get different action shots.

These are just some tips. Do not just take the bare minimum pictures to get your car listed. It makes a difference when you have professional-looking pictures because guest will be attracted to your listing. The good news is you do not have to break the bank to get professional-looking pictures.

Picking a Location for Your Photoshoot

Next, it is all about planning for your photoshoot. I highly recommend you do a photoshoot for your car at scenic areas such as golf courses, attractions, murals, sunrises, sunsets, or beaches. You want to put your car in different scenarios so guests can picture themselves driving your vehicle. As a tip, use different locations and not the basic pictures that other hosts take. People do not think outside of the box, and they take photos in their driveway or on the side of the street. Make sure yours stand out.

How Many Photos to List?

You want to list 20-30 pictures for your listings. My students take over 300 photos in their photoshoots. This gives them the ability to select the best ones with different locations and different angles of the car.

Types of Photos

There are different angles and photos you should take of your vehicle. You can take wide-angle photos, close-ups, and photos that show the features of the car. For my Tesla Model X, I have pictures with the doors all the way open. You want to take these types of action shots, the shots with the best look for your car. This separates you from the competition. If you have a 17-inch screen, you want pictures of that. Whatever features and upgraded accessories your car have, be sure to capture them.

Be also particular about the interior photos of the car you take. When car manufacturers like Tesla, Ford, or Acura showcase their cars, what type of photos do they take of their car's interior? You want yours to be of similar quality.

8. Set Up Payment

The setup for payments is easy and convenient. The payment is done through Stripe payment processing. If you do not currently have an account set up, it takes just minutes to set up and be verified.

9. Go Live

Once you publish your car, it will be listed. It is that easy. With the list I have given you in this chapter, prepare the items you will need beforehand in order to have a seamless account set up.

Here are some last tips for wrapping up this section on your listing.

- Update your calendar often. (Update once a week)
- Be responsive. (Be sure to respond within an hour)
- Add "Extras" (Car Seat, Toll Pass, Unlimited Miles)
- Offer discounts.
- Set minimum booked days.
- Set maximum booked days.

Visit Crfortunes.com to get access to my course that will teach you more secrets on car rentals. Use code "Noelle 40" for huge savings!

Car Description Examples

LUXURY MID TIER CARS

*** Clean and Sanitized***

Brand New [Insert Year Make and Model]

This [insert Model] will make people turn their heads! Perfect car for Florida weather!

NO SMOKING, NO PETS, NO OFF-ROADING!

It is well equipped inside and out, an eye catching (insert color)!

- Apple/Android Car Play
- Automatic Transmission/Manual Transmission
- Push Start
- Remote Start
- Power Windows

- Power Locks
- Keyless Entry
- Bluetooth
- 6 USB Ports
- Radio AM/FM/Satellite
- Tinted Windows
- Back Up Camera
- Add Additional Features

AND MUCH MORE!

DISCOUNTS AVAILABLE
X% Weekly
X% Monthly

If you have any questions, please do not hesitate to ask. I am quick to respond!

Local Pick Up in [INSERT CITY, STATE]. Contactless Delivery to [INSERT DELIVERY LOCATIONS] available!

THIS IS THE ACTUAL [insert Make] YOU WILL GET - NO BAIT AND SWITCH - THANKS FOR LOOKING

NO SMOKING
NO PETS
NO OFF-ROADING

CLEANING: I deliver all cars straight from being hand washed and detailed, meaning the car will be cleaned and sanitized prior to the start of your trip. You will be charged a cleaning fee if the

SETTING UP YOUR TURO ACCOUNT

[INSERT MAKE] is returned excessively dirty, meaning stains, excessive dust, mud (again NO OFF-ROADING of any kind is allowed), spilled drinks, smoke odor (NO SMOKING is allowed), pet/animal hairs (NO PETS allowed). Cleaning fees range from $30 to $50. If you smoke in this vehicle, charges can cost you up to $250.

TOLLS: Vehicle is equipped with a Sun Pass so you can go through Sun Pass/EZ Pass for your convenience! It is Pay Per Use. All charges will be applied at the end of your trip plus a $5 service charge.

GAS: Vehicle uses [INSERT FUEL TYPE] and will be full at the start of your trip. For your convenience, you can Prepay for gas so you can return the car at any fuel level. If car is not returned full, you will be charged to fill it up plus a $10 fee.

You're going to love this car!

<u>Electric Vehicles</u>

Oh, you are going to love this [INSERT MAKE] which seats [INSERT NUMBER OF PASSENGERS]! This [INSERT MAKE] is equipped with [INSERT HIGHLIGHTED FEATURE]! [INSERT DESCRIPTION OF HOW THE FEATURE WORKS]. Whether you want to take an extended test drive before buying, are heading on a road trip, or already own a [INSERT MODEL] and do not want anything else while on vacation, you will have a wonderful time in this [INSERT COLOR] [INSERT YEAR AND MODEL]. Driving a [INSERT MAKE] is a great experience, smooth ride and it feels like you are driving something from the future.

It is well equipped inside and out, an eye catching (insert color)!

- Autopilot
- [INSERT TOTAL RANGE]
- Supercharging
- [INSERT TYPE OF INTERIOR]
- Power Windows
- Power Locks
- Keyless Entry
- Bluetooth
- [INSERT NUMBER OF] USB Ports
- Radio AM/FM/Satellite
- Tinted Windows
- Back Up Camera
- All Glass Panoramic Roof
- Tech package (GPS navigation, presenting door handles when you approach, cornering headlights and more)
- Heated Front Seats
- Add Additional Features

Local Pick Up in [INSERT CITY, STATE]. Contactless Delivery to [INSERT DELIVERY LOCATIONS] available!

THIS IS THE ACTUAL [INSERT MAKE] YOU WILL GET - NO BAIT AND SWITCH - THANKS FOR LOOKING

NO SMOKING
NO PETS

CLEANING: I deliver all cars straight from being hand washed and detailed, meaning the car will be cleaned and sanitized prior

SETTING UP YOUR TURO ACCOUNT

to the start of your trip. You will be charged a cleaning fee if the [INSERT MAKE] is returned excessively dirty, meaning stains, excessive dust, mud (again NO OFF-ROADING of any kind is allowed), spilled drinks, smoke odor (NO SMOKING is allowed), pet/animal hairs (NO PETS allowed). Cleaning fees range from $30 to $50. If you smoke in this vehicle, charges can cost you up to $250.

TOLLS: Vehicle is equipped with a Sun Pass so you can go through Sun Pass/EZ Pass for your convenience! It is Pay Per Use. All charges will be applied at the end of your trip plus a $5 service charge.

CHARGING: Vehicle can be charged at a Supercharger or at you home and will be full at the start of your trip. For your convenience, you can Prepay for charging so you can return the car at any fuel level. If car is not returned fully charged, you will be charged to fill it up plus a $10 fee.

You're going to love this car!

Sports/Exotic Vehicles

The [INSERT MAKE AND MODEL] is an extremely capable high-performance sports car. Perfect for your vacation and business needs in and around the Orlando area, we guarantee you will be turning heads in this beauty. The [INSERT NUMBER OF PASSENGERS] vehicle gives you those vacation vibes that you should expect from [INSERT MAKE] through its performance and aesthetic. The [INSERT ENGINE SIZE] provides the perfect amount of power and gives off a beautiful roar from the engine. You can't go wrong by picking the [INSERT MODEL]!

It is well equipped inside and out, an eye catching (insert color)!

- Apple/Android Car Play
- Automatic Transmission/Manual Transmission
- Push Start
- Remote Start
- Power Windows
- Power Locks
- Keyless Entry
- Bluetooth
- 6 USB Ports
- Radio AM/FM/Satellite
- Tinted Windows
- Back Up Camera
- Add Additional Features

AND MUCH MORE!

Local Pick Up in [INSERT CITY, STATE]. Contactless Delivery to [INSERT DELIVERY LOCATIONS] available!

THIS IS THE ACTUAL [insert Make] YOU WILL GET - NO BAIT AND SWITCH - THANKS FOR LOOKING

NO SMOKING
NO PETS
NO OFF-ROADING

CLEANING: I deliver all cars straight from being hand washed and detailed, meaning the car will be cleaned and sanitized prior to the start of your trip. You will be charged a cleaning fee if the

SETTING UP YOUR TURO ACCOUNT

[INSERT MAKE] is returned excessively dirty, meaning stains, excessive dust, mud (again NO OFF-ROADING of any kind is allowed), spilled drinks, smoke odor (NO SMOKING is allowed), pet/animal hairs (NO PETS allowed). Cleaning fees range from $30 to $50. If you smoke in this vehicle, charges can cost you up to $250.

TOLLS: Vehicle is equipped with a Sun Pass so you can go through Sun Pass/EZ Pass for your convenience! It is Pay Per Use. All charges will be applied at the end of your trip plus a $5 service charge.

GAS: Vehicle uses [INSERT FUEL TYPE] and will be full at the start of your trip. For your convenience, you can Prepay for gas so you can return the car at any fuel level. If car is not returned full, you will be charged to fill it up plus a $10 fee.

You're going to love this car!

CHAPTER IV

RENTING YOUR VEHICLE

The Race is Not Over Because I Have Not Won Yet.
Anonymous

Next, let's discuss the proper pricing structure for your vehicle so you can price your cars and get the most bookings. When it comes down to pricing your car, let me give you a word of advice. First, do not try to be the cheapest on the market. Remember, you are in business and want to make a profit. And not only should you pay attention to the cost you are charging for your car, but you also have to consider the mileage and wear and tear on the vehicle, especially a luxury car.

I want you to understand that it is not just about the numbers or payouts you receive. The actual profit and loss will determine what you must pay to keep the vehicle serviced. I will continue to reiterate how excellent this platform is for creating income. Still, I also want you to keep in the back of your mind what it truly costs to maintain and upkeep your vehicle and run your business.

Currently, my students are averaging $500 - $1,500 profit per car. Of course, this variation is based on the type of vehicle. My economy cars make on average $800-900 a month. Luxury cars like my Tesla and Range Rover can average $2,000- $3,000 per month.

Book Instantly

After listing your vehicle, the next thing to know about is bookings. When we coach students on their listings, we advise them not to secure any listing using the "Book Instantly" feature when starting the business. This is a setting that automatically accepts a guest's booking in your vehicle without your having to approve the trip manually or vet your renter. However, when you set up your account, there is an option to disable this feature.

When you first begin, I highly recommend not taking instant bookings because you want enough time to ensure the car is ready and in the best condition possible.

Vetting Your Renter

Before you accept a booking take the time to vet your guests to ensure you are receiving the best booking and the renter is a responsible driver. Vetting does not take much time because it is only a conversation. However, this extra inquiry shows the renter that you are a serious business owner. As a result, it may deter any renter that may not be a good fit and can lessen the chances of renting to a reckless driver.

When they request to book your car, you should ask them some questions such as:

- What is their name?
- What is the purpose of the rental?
- Will any other guests be in the car?
- Is this a local trip or will you be traveling?

You can also vet a guest by checking their reviews. If they have rented before on Turo and brought the car back dirty or mishandled the rental, the other host will mention this in the review. Use reviews to your advantage. I have denied requests to reduce the risk of my car because I read bad reviews from previous hosts.

The goal of vetting is to minimize the risk of your cars being damaged by bad guests. You only want to deal with great guests. If a guest does not have reviews, use your best judgment to accept or deny the request.

Car Details

At the end of this chapter, you will find a Car Wish list where you will insert your car payment, car insurance, and your utilities to help you determine the minimum amount to list your car. There is also a resource that I have provided where you can plug in your car details to help you navigate pricing your car.

Dream Rental

Every host should have a dream rental price for their vehicle. The dream rental pricing, on average, is 2.5 to 3 times your minimum. Your minimum pricing will be your car payment divided by the expected occupancy rate. The dream rental price will give you a range of what you will be charging for your car(s).

For example, if your minimum price is $40 and your dream price is $120. You can research your competitors' prices and find what they are charging as a point of reference. It is okay if your dream price exceeds your competitors' price. You can charge more depending on your car's size, the year, and/or the model of your car. Newer cars can be listed for more. You can charge less for deliveries or your daily rate to be competitive. Also, your pricing will change due to holidays and events happening in your area. Remember, this is your business, so you can determine if you want to charge more based on your dream rental.

Car Wish List

In the next section you will find a template you can use to help you price your cars, so you are not leaving money on the table. You will find plug-in areas where you can insert numbers to help you with the calculations.

TURO™ MILLIONAIRE SECRETS

Car Rental Fortunes Book Activities

Car	Price	Turo Daily Rate

Daily Price Calculator

For this calculation you'll need your monthly car payments, car insurance, average occupancy (projected), and car utilities (monthly car wash, accessories, and monthly maintenance). You will also need to do some research on Turo and Car Rental Companies (Avis, Budget, Enterprise) to see how your competition is pricing similar vehicles.

Car Details	Amount
Car Payment	
Car Insurance	
Utilities	
Avg Occupancy	

Once you input these numbers into this formula:

(Car Payment + Car Insurance + Utilities) / Average (Avg) Occupancy = Daily Price

First, you'll need to understand what your average occupancy is. I use an 80% occupancy for my projections. The average month has 30 days and if I'm using 80% for my calculations, I have to multiply 30 days by 0.8 which equals 24 days. Now that you know how to calculate your average occupancy, you can use the equation above.

Use the space below to find your minimum daily price.

(_____ + _____ + _____) / _____ = _____

You have calculated your minimum daily rate to break even with your new rental, however, we're not here to just break even. We're here to run a successful sustainable business! Let's take our minimum daily price and multiply that by 2.5.

Min Daily Price x 2.5 = Dream Price

_____ x 2.5 = _____

Now that we've created a range for our prices, a price we can't go below for our car and a second price we can go up to or even above depending on what you'll find out in the next step in your research. I've created a table for you to fill in with data you've found. Below is that table. Research 10 cars on Turo and 10 cars on various Car rental companies. Make sure they are comparable in size (for the rental companies). Include Model and Year in your Turo cars. Make sure these cars are within the last 5 years.

RENTING YOUR VEHICLE

Turo	Price	Car Rental Comp	Price

Do not worry in your calculations if the cars are newer than your car. It gives you a clearer perspective on what you can charge for your car. Just so you know, not all new cars perform as well as older cars. This will come down to your pictures and what your car offers.

Car Feature List

Create a list of the features your car has that would stand out to your guests. This will help you with your listing by making it easier to pick some stand out points for your car. Guests do read your listings and the better it is, the more you'll stand out.

Car Features

RENTING YOUR VEHICLE

CAR RENTAL CALCULATOR		Minimum Rental $37	Dream Rental $92	Potential Profit Range $792 $1,325	
CAR DETAILS	VALUES	PRICE RANGE	TOTALS	BREAKDOWN	TOTALS
Car Payment	$ 450.00	Total Car Payments	$883	Avg Turo Daily	$1,675
Car Insurance	$ 160.00	Base Daily Rental	$37	Dream Daily	$2,208
Car Utilities	$ 273.00	Dream Daily Rental	$92		
Avg Occupancy	80%	Average Turo Rental*	$ 69.78		
		Average Car Rental**	$ 90.11		

*Average Turo Rental = Cars listed on Turo that are similar to your vehicle (at least 8 comparable vehicles)

**Average Car Rental = Cars listed by Rental Agencies that are similar to your vehicle (at least 8 comparable vehicles)

CAR UTILITIES	COST
Car Wash (monthly)	$ 68.00
Assessories	$ 175.00
Maintaince	$ 30.00

TURO CARS	PRICE	RENTAL CARS	PRICE
2013 Altima	$ 75.00	Compact	$ 99.00
2019 Altima	$ 60.00	Compact	$ 93.00
2020 Altima	$ 40.00	Compact	$ 116.00
2012 Altima	$ 38.00	Midsize	$ 48.00
2020 Altima	$ 79.00	Midsize	$ 86.00
2020 Altima	$ 89.00	Midsize	$ 82.00
2021 Altima	$ 69.00	Midsize	$ 94.00
2020 Altima	$ 89.00	Midsize	$ 91.00
2019 Altima	$ 89.00	Compact	$ 102.00

CHAPTER V

CHECK-IN AND CHECK-OUT PROCESS

> *"Someone is sitting in the shade today because someone planted a tree a long time ago."*
> Warren Buffet

The check-in and check-out process is integral to your guest's experience. It is also essential to your business because it allows you to protect your assets- your cars. In addition, how well you document the trip can determine whether you receive your reimbursements from Turo or, should any car damage or an accident occurs.

Check-in Process

For the check-in process, you want to keep a few main areas at the forefront.

>   #1) The cleanliness and appearance of your car
>   #2) Proper documentation
>   #3) The Customer Experience

Let's begin with the appearance of your vehicles. Maintaining your car's upkeep is a reflection of your business. A good business owner takes pride in its products and does what is necessary to ensure its customers are happy with their rental. Your car should always be clean when your customer rents from you. This is non-negotiable. And although it is not necessary to have the car professionally cleaned, I feel it is always a nice touch for each reservation. Cleaning your car and sanitizing goes a long way, and your renter will appreciate it.

Because car washes will be an ongoing business expense, shop around to ensure you get a good deal for these. You may find an option where you can pay a monthly fee which will offer you savings.

Before Pick Up

After your car is cleaned and detailed is a good time to take photos of the car. I generally take pre-trip photos starting 24 hours before the trip. During this process, take many car pictures from all angles. Having photos from every angle is important because if anything happens like damages, scratches, accidents, etc., you can have damages reimbursed from the guest or Turo, depending on the damage. Also, when you document everything, it increases the chances that your claim will be approved. Turo will instantly support it with the proper evidence if you have documented proof. If you try to put in a claim without proof, Turo will deny it.

Included at the end of this chapter is the type of pictures you should take of your vehicle. Feel free to use this as a checklist and use it each time your car is rented. It will also come in handy when you have staff managing your fleet.

Before you hand the vehicle over to the guest, make sure your vehicle is in great working condition regardless of how old it is. This means there should be no oil lights on, no check engine light on, and the air conditioning is working, etc. Also, make sure the tires are good and the vehicle senses are fully functioning on the car. This should go without saying; however, some simple things are often overlooked.

Check-out Process

I take just as many pictures as the check-in process for my check-out process. I can take anywhere between 60-80 photos of my cars. It is very important to document the aftermath of every trip.

Car Pick Up and Delivery

When your guests pick up the car, remind them to take pre-trip photos because they feel more obligated to pay those reimbursements if anything happens. It is even easier for you to win those claims if they also have those photos.

Contactless Drop-Off

Since the pandemic, I have incorporated contactless deliveries. I want my guests to be safe and my staff to be safe.

Keep Trip Records

You have 24 hours to upload all photos before and after the trip. If you miss that window, Turo will not cover the reimbursements, so it is imperative you do this.

Things that you want to make sure you have taken pictures (records) of are:

- The mileage
- Gas
- Car interior & exterior
- Tire thread
- Any other area on your car not listed above, i.e., specialty rims, car grill, etc.

I will share a true story from one of my coaches, KJ Steir. He rented out his Tesla Model X, and the guest drove 400 miles over what they paid. He was supposed to receive $60 every mile over, but because he did not properly document the trip with post-trip photos, he essentially lost out.

Toll Charges

Not only do I upload pictures, but in Florida, we have a sun pass that allows any tolls to be charged directly to the account holder. This is convenient for guests but can also be an overlooked expense. On the SunPass website, I take a picture of the exact dates of their trips to show all charges for reimbursement. In addition, if I pay any garage fees or parking, I also take photos and document them. You have 24 hours to upload your documentation.

Car Return

When the renter returns your vehicle, you want to ensure it is dropped off at the agreed location. With the GPS trackers in your car, you will know where the car is and not have to stress about the location. For some cars, I have an option to pick them up, but it depends on the vehicle.

Reimbursements

The best thing about getting your reimbursements is that Turo makes it extremely easy after the trip when you provide proof of requested reimbursement items. They also offer an additional 60 to 90 days if the driver accrued a speeding ticket, a parking ticket, or any violation received while the car was in their possession. You can go after your guests for reimbursements once you upload all your evidence.

Turo will reimburse additional items, including a super dirty vehicle and any smoking by guests. The renter has the option to elect cleaning as an upgrade. If they choose not to select this, however, this can be reimbursed if the car is returned dirty. Again, this is why your check-in and check-out pictures are so important. If you find any proof that there was smoking or smells like smoke, they will have to cover this. Turo strictly prohibits smoking in any of the cars, and it is relatively easy to seek reimbursements from guests if they break these rules.

You can also be reimbursed for guests if you must refill the car. If it is an electric vehicle, you are reimbursed if you must charge the vehicle.

Reimbursement List

- ✓ Gas
- ✓ Tolls
- ✓ EV Charging
- ✓ Additional Miles
- ✓ Cleaning
- ✓ Smoking
- ✓ Wheel Damage

What Turo Will Not Reimburse

Although Turo is generous with reimbursements, there are some things they will not cover. One of the main things is recalls. They will allow you to list the cars that have recalls; however, if you do not fix those recalls before anything happens, Turo will not reimburse you, and they may remove you from the platform altogether.

CHECK-IN AND CHECK-OUT PROCESS

Although they will allow you to list the cars, they want you to make sure the customer is safe. They trust your judgment, but they will investigate the claim. If they find anything wrong, you will be dropped from the platform. If you have any recall issues, take care of them as soon as possible. Do not put yourself or others at risk.

Photo Checklist

To begin, take six wide angles going around the car: front, side, back, another side, then the four angles combining two sides simultaneously.

Next, take a photo of each tire tread with the tread depth reader in the photo; this shows the tires are in excellent condition before the guest rents the reader. A word of caution. If your tires are under 4/32" of remaining tread depth, get them changed. This qualifies your tires as bald. If a guest reports this, Turo will investigate and remove you from the platform if they find it accurate or anywhere close to a non-safe factor. You can purchase a tread depth reader on Amazon or your local auto store.

Lastly, take multiple pictures, capturing every panel to document no damage to each car panel.

The photos you take of your car should include the following:

Exterior

- Eight Wide Angles of the Car
- Left Front and Side
- Front

- Right Front and Side
- Driver Side
- Back Left and Side
- Back
- Back Right and Side
- Passenger Side
- Tires
- One without depth tread
- One with depth tread reading
- Close-Ups
- Three pictures of the bumper
- One from each angle (left, front, right)
- Each panel
- Panel over front tire
- Driver door
- Back driver door
- Panel over back driver side tire
- Back bumper
- One from each angle (left, front, right)
- Panel over back passenger side tire
- Back passenger door
- Passenger door

Interior

- Driver seat
- Passenger seat
- Back seat
- From both sides
- Trunk
- Each door frame

CHECK-IN AND CHECK-OUT PROCESS

- 1 close up
- 1 full door
- 1 from a low angle

Visit Crfortunes.com to get access to my course that will teach you more secrets on car rentals. Use code "Noelle 40" for huge savings!

CHAPTER VI
PROTECTING YOUR VEHICLE

> "*Focus on Your Goal, Do not Look in Any Direction but Ahead.*"
> Noelle Randall

As a business owner, you should protect your car with insurance. Turo requires that "US hosts should check their state laws for specific registration requirements. Most states require that hosts demonstrate "financial responsibility" to register their car. This is satisfied by having personal car insurance. It is your choice whether to use Turo's additional coverage. I suggest you have a commercial policy with full coverage for your vehicles, as the insurance made available through Turo may not satisfy that requirement. I also have commercial insurance and coverage with Turo.

If you decide to get a commercial policy, I suggest getting quotes through an insurance broker so they can suggest what coverage is needed. Visit a local insurance broker, and they can compare coverages and pricing to ensure you secure the best deal possible. That is the best way to ensure you get the best coverage, even for commercial policies. Also, ensure you have a 'For Hire' use coverage in your policy. Choose what option works best for you. If anything happens, you want to ensure you are fully reimbursed for the damages without any delays or disruptions to your business. Also note, commercial insurance is required for exotic and high-end luxury cars.

There are five types of insurance coverages for your vehicle. There's comprehensive coverage, liability, personal injury, uninsured and underinsured motorist coverage, and collision.

Comprehensive Coverage

This type of coverage covers the vehicle if something happens to your vehicle, and it is not your fault. For example, if there is a fire outbreak, non-collision, or a tree falling on your vehicle due to the wind, weather, hail, etc.

Liability Insurance

Liability insurance is a requirement on every personal or commercial policy. "Liability coverage has two components:

- **Bodily injury liability** may help pay for costs related to another person's injuries if you cause an accident.

- **Property damage liability** may help pay for damage you cause to another person's property while driving."

Personal Injury Protection

Personal injury is not mandatory; however, I suggest you carry it. It covers your medical bills, hospital visit, emergency rooms, or anything related to your injury if you are injured in an accident. It also protects you from paying out of pocket for your medical bills. Although you may have excellent medical insurance, if you are injured you will not have to use your medical insurance, and your bills will be paid by the car insurance company instead.

Uninsured and Underinsured Motorist Coverage

Uninsured insurance covers you if you are involved in an accident and the guilty party doesn't stay on the scene, or they do not have any coverage of their own. It protects you from having to pay out of pocket for those damages. Companies such as GEICO,

Allstate, and Progressive offer this coverage. Check with your state to determine if this is required coverage. However, even if it is not required, I recommend having this insurance. If your vehicle is damaged by a hit-and-run, Turo will not cover that expense.

Collision Coverage

Collision coverage helps pay to repair or replace your vehicle if it is damaged or destroyed in an accident with another car, regardless of who is at fault. Even if you are at fault, your insurance company will pay for damages after you pay your deductible.

Protection From Theft

Do what is necessary to secure your vehicle(s). As I mentioned earlier, I have trackers on my cars. I even took it a step further by having a GPS tracker with a kill switch, which means the engine will not start if I do not activate it. Trackers are worth having installed in your vehicle. I will advise you to have a few ways to protect your vehicle against theft just in case someone disables one of them; you still have another way to find and secure your vehicle. This includes not only tracking systems but having spare car keys as well. Think about it this way. If someone does steal your vehicle, once you track it down, you can access the vehicle without having a physical confrontation. If your car is stolen on a trip with a guest, since you know who the guest is, Turo will cover this. They will go after them to apprehend the car. Additionally, if your car is stolen on a trip with a guest, since you know who the guest is, Turo will cover this. They will go after them to apprehend the car.

Lastly, consider securing Turo's premium coverage, which has no deductible. The policy will compensate you for lost rental fees and provide a replacement vehicle while yours is being repaired. In my opinion, it is worth the cost. Turo is the best-rated opportunity in this category.

CHAPTER VII

CAR ACQUISITION AND FINANCING

"Today is your opportunity to build the tomorrow you want."
Ken Poirot

As with any business venture, you must fully understand your bandwidth or what you can manage. When you start building your fleet, one thing you do not want to do is acquire too many cars, especially if you do not have the staff or the money to maintain the cars. This will set you up for business failure. My advice is to start with a manageable amount of cars. Once you build up your fleet of economy, high-end, and luxury cars, you will have to hire staff to maintain these cars. So make sure you build your fleet wisely. Do not put yourself in too much debt. I am not saying to be scared to pick up that debt, but you do not want to over-extend yourself and put yourself in a position to fail. If you only can start with two or three cars in the beginning, so be it. First, learn the business, how to market and keep a steady cash flow with every car each month, and work your way up.

When you start building your fleet, you have a few options. Those options are cash cars, leasing, equity-based loan, vehicle financing, and joint ventures, as discussed in chapter 2. You can use some of these options or incorporate them all over time.

Building Your Fleet with Cash Cars

I recommend you first start with economy cars. In fact, cash cars are a great place to find these types of cars, so you do not have to break the bank for them. You can find some absolute gems in places like OfferUp, Facebook Marketplace, and local dealers. Your local mom-and-pop dealers will also sell cars for cheaper. These cars can be listed on apps like GetAround and HyreCar. For the sake of this book and the Turo platform, if the cars do not have any recalls, you can list them on Turo. Economy cars can rent between $300- $400, and you can quickly profit from $1200 to $1600 a month. And because you paid cash for the car, everything you make will be a profit.

Lease

A lease is one way to get a luxury or high-end model but to be honest, I do not necessarily recommend a lease because of the mileage restrictions and a few other stipulations. However, if you decide to lease a car, check if you can rent them on different platforms. Also, depending on the type of car, you will have to accurately manage this in your listings if you can put it on a car-sharing platform.

There are a few benefits to leasing. Some benefits of a lease are:

- It will not appear on your credit report.
- You can get a newer make and model every few years. With a lease, you can keep it for the length of the lease, trade it in, and make more money on the newer car. You can keep doing this for however long you choose and still make money.
- The maintenance is covered.

Equity-Based Loan

An equity-based loan is when you have money but do not have credit. With an equity-based loan, you put down 20 to 50 percent of the car's value with a low monthly payment. I only recommend this for established businesses having a two-plus years credit history. With this option, the risk is very high. On the other hand, one benefit of an equity-based loan is purchasing exotic cars such as a

Lamborghini, BMW I8, or Rolls-Royce for less than you would usually pay.

Financing Your Vehicles

Once you start building your business, you have the option to finance your cars under your company. This applies whether you have good credit or not. Financing is when you use or leverage your credit to obtain money on terms from a bank or financial institution. Financing terms are usually 60, 72, or 84 months, depending on your credit score.

The first step to financing is building the perfect credit portfolio. However, you can finance with not-so-stellar credit if you want to work on increasing your score for the most favorable rates. Because I have built my credit portfolio, I have been able to finance cars like Tesla with no money down. I know what it is like to be on both sides of the FICO score, and once you apply what is presented in this chapter, you'll be able to do the same things I am doing.

You want to aim for 720 or better for the best interest rates. This is how you get the best rates, no matter what bank you approach, and they will offer you a loan without any money down. You can take that pre-approval and get whatever car you want with financing. You only want to finance cars you do not have enough money to purchase, and you know you can get a higher return.

Exotic Car Financing

You can also finance exotic cars with favorable terms. The lender will give you many months to pay off the vehicle, so you will have a respectable monthly payment. With exotic cars, you will want to have your credit over 700. That is the perfect spot to be so you can have those zero-down payments. Some banks may not do that for you when financing exotic vehicles, those cars that are over $150k. However, some banks, like JJ Bank and Woodside Credit, will offer you all 144-month credit.

Joint Ventures

I want to continue the discussion regarding joint ventures from chapter two. As I stated before, a joint venture is an agreement between you and one or more parties that indicates you will do business together under one entity after you draw up suitable terms.

An example of a joint venture is:

You may split the profit 50/50. Or, you conduct the leg work while your business partner is a silent partner and offers use of his financial resources.

Joint venturing is a great way to get started, and they are very profitable for those who may not have good credit or money. They are also accessible to those who may have good credit and cash but do not have the time to do so.

Visit Crfortunes.com to get access to my course that will teach you more secrets on car rentals. Use code "Noelle 40" for huge savings!

CHAPTER VIII

LEAD EXPLOSION: MARKETING

> "*Marketing is Not Anyone's Job, It's Everyone's Job.*"
> Jack Welch

Now let's dive into marketing aspect of your Turo business and what marketing efforts to use to increase your car rental revenue. Marketing may not be your forte, but it is just as important as having your listing set up. Sales and marketing are the lifelines to your business, so please make sure you put a strategy in place. To be effective in marketing, you must be consistent. You also need to have a budget in place to cover the cost of ads and promotions. I suggest you invest at least one-third of your profits into your marketing budget to increase your revenue and visibility.

There are various strategies for marketing using different platforms. Some of them include Instagram, Facebook, and Google. All three platforms have different types of accounts you can set up. With Google, you must first verify your business to place ads. With Instagram and Facebook, you must create your ad accounts, and you can run ads directly from your profile. Make sure you set up a business account to access the business account features. When you use relevant hashtags and targeted ads, your post will appear on your targeted audience's timeline. That is how you use targeted ads based on your analytics.

Once you are consistently posting daily, you can start running ads on Facebook or Instagram. I suggest you have a basic understanding of how to manage and understand the analytics. You do not have to be a whiz at understanding the analytics, but you should learn what the analytics mean to analyze what marketing creates the best ROI. Knowing your analytics will also help you when you hire staff by reducing the learning curve.

Another platform you can utilize is Yelp! There are so many amazing opportunities to grow your business with marketing. With so many options available, you can also use Linktree to help you organize your links. For example, if you have YouTube, Twitter, and other social media, Linktree allows you to have all your links in one place, so when someone clicks on it, they can either go to your website or your Turo platform, or other social media channels.

Using Social Media

If you're not good at using social media, you can outsource it. Instead, hire a social media manager that can manage your pages effectively. They will help you create a content plan and calendar that you can use to post daily and draw attention to your business. On Instagram and Facebook, post consistently. I have some students that post up to 12 times a day.

Your marketing should be creative. With social media, you can use Memes, TikTok videos, reels, and anything else that is trending. If you have a social media account, you have most likely seen fun memes, and challenges. Take advantage of these free marketing tools. People will see your memes, and they will want to connect with you before you know it.

Using Shorts

Another way you can market is by creating small videos. Shorts are 20 to 30-second videos you can use to showcase your car's features. For my Tesla, I showcase the Falcon doors going up. Creating these short videos sparks the interest of those who want to rent my cars. These are not like explainer videos, but short videos with trending music are easy to get people to click on your vehicles, especially if you're using Facebook and Instagram.

Google Verified

If you want to be found in numerous places, Google Verified is one way to get listed. Because Google is not just a search engine; it is an ad agency, you'll be able to run ads through Google.

Steps to Getting Verified

1. Sign into your Google Account or create one.
2. Enter the name of your business. You may also be able to select your business from the list of suggested businesses.
3. Search for and select a business category.
4. Choose whether you have a location customers can visit.
5. Enter the service area of your business.
6. Enter a phone number and website URL.
7. Select a verification option- verify now, verify later. Review your information before you request verification.

A few additional tips. When you list your business, give the necessary information and provide pictures if you can. After registration, they will send you a postcard in the mail with a verification number. Enter this in Google Verified to become registered as a business. Upon verification, you will be rewarded with credits to start running ads.

Email Marketing

Email lists are still a massive way to get in front of more people. An email list is composed of emails provided by people who have shown interest in a particular promotion offered. Some companies have a list of 20,000 to 30,000, and you can pay to get your ad and marketing material into their campaign. Or you can start to capture emails through your websites. If you are using your website or lead page, the best way to get people to sign up is to offer discounts, promotions, or free information.

Lifestyle Marketing

Do not underestimate the power of lifestyle marketing. One of the biggest draws to luxury and exotic car marketing is that people want to see themselves experiencing what it is like to drive in one of those cars. You can implement this same type of marketing using your vehicles by driving in scenic areas or the city.

You can utilize the short video format to promote your car better than just using a static image with some words. Videos keep people's attention; it makes them want to click and learn more. Because of the high engagement for videos, they should be included in your marketing game plan. You do not need expensive equipment and can use your iPhone on Android to get started. Videos can consist of video footage, or you use a photo slide show with nice backgrounds and murals. Allow your creativity to run wild. Keeping your potential clients engaged will lead them to reach out and book you.

Using the analytics mentioned earlier will help you determine what people are engaging with, which you can use to direct your marketing strategy. You want to give your customers more of what they want to see. If you know a particular video or type of video draws more attention, make more videos like that. Then start using targeted ads with those videos to get more people to click on your link. It is that easy to generate leads.

Guest Reviews

One of the best and fastest easy to grow your business is with guest reviews. Remember, Turo is modeled after Airbnb, and guest reviews are a big deal. Reviews can be the deciding factor in whether or not your vehicle is booked. Do not be afraid to ask your guest for reviews. You are a customer service business and need those reviews to show other guests that you are the best choice. I am a super host, and I still ask for reviews. I even offer them incentives.

The best time for reviews is when guests have ended their trip and have enjoyed it. You can request reviews through the app, contact your guests directly, or ask them in person. If I ask them in person, I may waive specific fees up to a certain amount because I want the written reviews. That is more important to me than the ten bucks in tolls.

In addition to written reviews, video reviews are also great for marketing. A simple 10- or 15-seconds testimonial about a guest's experience will go a long way, especially when you post to your social media. People love to see testimonials.

Review Incentives and Discounts

Turo allows you to send past guests discount codes, so if you want, you can send incentives for video reviews. Another incentive program can be for your loyal customers. For example, you can consider giving a discount to customers that consistently make direct bookings with you.

LEAD EXPLOSION: MARKETING

Whatever your marketing strategy, remember you must show up consistently and be credible in the marketplace.

CHAPTER IX

DIVERSIFY YOUR PORTFOLIO

"Diversification is a protection against ignorance. It makes very little sense for those who know what they're doing."
Warren Buffett

Diversifying your portfolio is not a one-trick pony. It entails marketing your cars, adding a variety of cars to your fleet, and still being profitable no matter which platforms you list your car on. This chapter is for those who have acquired a fleet of cars and want to diversify their portfolio.

The benefit of diversifying your portfolio is to profit from various car platforms. Let me explain why this is important. Turo is one of the leading platforms for you to share your car. As they're the originators, the types of cars that do best on this platform are luxury, high-end, and exotic cars. Although economy cars can also do well, Turo is more geared towards luxury and high-end cars. Other platforms like HyreCar and GetAround are more geared towards economy cars. On these platforms, you can rent out your cars weekly, and you can do well with Honda Civics, Honda Accords, Toyota Camrys, Nissans, etc.

If you have an F-150 or work van, there are apps where you can make money by listing these types of vehicles and helping people move and rent them instead of going to places like U-Haul, Home Depot, or Lowe's to rent a truck. Instead, they can rent a nicer truck from you instead of paying movers, which can get pretty pricey.

These are just a few examples of diversifying your portfolio without having to do anything different on each platform, using the cars you already own. However, I must add this disclaimer. Before you join any of these platforms:

1. Test it out.

2. Rent the car, use the apps, see how the platform works, and use that experience to make the processes easier for you.
3. Learn the ins and outs and talk to other hosts.

Versatility

Lastly, I want to share how to adapt to your current market for the highest returns. There are times when you may have to be versatile to make a profit. As you learn, understand, and adjust to what your market wants, you carve out your niche to make a profit. Use your cars for what people in your area are interested in. For example, let's say Turo is not as popular in your area, but GetAround is. In that market, you know that people are not as interested in high-value cars. What you would do in that case is add more economy cars to your fleet. The market will let you know what it wants. It is your job as a business owner to adjust your business to make maximum profit.

If car rental platforms are unavailable for you, and you have high-value cars like Porsche, BMW, I8, Lamborghinis, or Rolls-Royce, and you want to secure more options, start to network with other businesses. You can sign a marketing contract with them and let them put their removable logo, hashtag, Instagram, website, or URL on your car, and you can market with their logo and business. High-value cars attract attention, which will cause people to check out the business information while checking out the car. It is a win-win situation; you're drawing leads to their business and getting paid. But, again, make sure all branding is removable, not permanent.

You can use your cars for other business ventures like allowing people to rent and take photoshoots with them. You can adjust by taking advantage of the events coming to your city. If you are in a town where there is always a major annual event, party, or whatever holidays are coming, pay attention to these dates. If you know your market has a specific holiday or local tradition coming up, it may not even be in your city; you can take your car down to the town and let them rent it out from there. If you are close enough, you can transport cars and charge higher fees than you usually would because of these events, and you can make more money. Here is the thing: I increase my price a bit when the holidays come around. So, for example, when Christmas or Halloween comes around, I rent my car because more tourists come into town, and I raise my prices to match the demand.

These tips help you adapt to your market to make more profits regardless of your area.

CHAPTER X

CREDIT REPAIR

> *Success doesn't come from what you do occasionally. It comes from what you do consistently."*
> Marie Forleo

In this section, you'll learn about credit repair. Working on your credit will be highly beneficial in helping you run your business without needing to tap into your cash reserves. When I first started in business, I didn't have good credit. As a result, it was difficult to grow my business because I was self-funding everything and, many times, was forced to bootstrap. Cleaning up my credit and applying for credit cards and business loans allowed me to achieve my growth goals. In this chapter, let's review some tips to help you improve your credit.

The first step is your credit sweep. This is where you begin, but also keep in mind you must be strategic in how you do this. So, before you start filing disputes, do it in this order.

1. Update your address with all three bureaus' credit bureaus to create unverifiable accounts that may be linked to an old address.
2. Report your highest-paying job. Do not report multiple jobs because it will not benefit you. You only want to report on the job that pays you most.
3. Suppress these third-party companies that report to the credit bureaus. You may not have known this, but the credit bureaus do not fact-check all the information they get. Instead, they pay third-party companies to verify your information to make their job easier. You can stop these third-party companies from verifying your information to make it harder for the credit bureaus to do so.

The five companies that record your information for the credit bureaus are

1. Core Logic
2. LexisNexis
3. Sage stream
4. ARS
5. Inavis

Reach out to these individual companies and opt-out of recording your information. Once you do that, this is part of prepping your credit report to get the collections, derogatory marks, and missed payments off your report.

The CFPB stands for Consumer Financial Protection Bureau, and it is a government agency that regulates credit bureaus. When you start filing for these disputes, you will use them to help you in your credit sweep.

How to File Disputes

Use an introductory dispute letter. This dispute letter is essentially just a challenge to the accuracy of these accounts listing all the accounts on your credit report that you want to be removed, including collections, charge-offs, repossessions, late payments, etc. Once they come back, verified or not, you can use letters like a 609 or MOV letter (Method of Verification) to challenge these accounts further. You will find one at the end of this chapter for use.

Building a Better Credit Report

Once you have the negative accounts removed from your credit report, it is time to build and create a positive credit report. To build a good credit report, you will need a good standing primary account and have up to three accounts aged four to five years. However, there's another way to build your credit. This is personal, not for business. One of the ways you know is through a secured credit card; although that is somewhat half step, it is better to have your money in your book than to get a secured loan.

To achieve this, you need ten positive accounts aged four to five years minimum, under 10% utilization, zero derogatory marks, and no more than two to three inquiries about accessing funds.

How to Get Good Standing Accounts Fast

Let's say you have three banks, Bank A, B, and C. Use $500 to open a savings account with a bank number A. It may not be the bank of your choice or credit, but you open that first bank account with Bank A. The next step is to take out a secured loan from the bank. Essentially, they will give your money to the bank in a loan. Now you have a payment that is due. After you have received the loan, use that money in Bank B, open another bank account, and get another secured loan in Bank B. Lastly, you'll repeat the same process for Bank C. If you do this correctly, you will have three good-standing accounts with good payments. Again, you are just using the same money over and over to create three good-standing accounts on top of the ones you may already have.

Add Primary Accounts

A primary account is simply an account that is solely based on your credit and your ability to repay that loan or account. You want to have more good-standing primary accounts to build on to help increase your credit score.

You can have good-standing accounts through RentReporters or Rental Kharma. For example, the rent you have been paying for your apartment, home, or primary residence can be used as an active account for your credit report. You can list it and even backdate it for up to two years. The company will check with the person receiving your rent to ensure the reports are correct; it is very easy and straightforward. This is an easy way to build good-standing accounts to boost your credit score.

Companies like Credit Builders allow you to report other trade lines like credit cards, phone lines, and other active trade lines on your credit report to help you build a good-looking portfolio or credit report.

Authorized Users

An authorized user is another way of building good credit. Someone came up with a brilliant idea to allow others to be benefactors of their good credit. With this, you can have friends or family members add you to their high limit and good standing aged years accounts to help boost your credit quickly. The best thing about an authorized user is that you do not have access to these cards, you are simply allowed to report this on your credit report, and that is the benefit of being able to do so.

When someone allows you to become an authorized user on their account, you want to have a specific goal that you are working towards so you are not adding accounts without a plan.

Applying for Business Credit

To get business credit, you need to put yourself in a positive position by removing the negative reports from building a better one. A good credit score allows you to get access to more funding. This is key to ensuring your business survives.

High Utilization

To build healthy credit, monitor your credit card utilization. Although this may seem like a Herculean task, it is possible and achievable.

To do so, you need to pay attention to the following dates:

- First is the due date; The due date is when you must make a payment. Never miss it because this is how you keep your payment history high; always make sure you're paying before or on the due date to ensure your account has a good standing.
- The next date to note is the closing date. The closing date is important because this is when your billing cycle ends. At the end of the closing date, the balance that has been spent will be reported for the due date. So, the balance you have to pay on that date is what they're going to report.
- Lastly, the last date to note is the reporting date. The reporting date and the closing date are not the same. You

must pay attention to the reporting dates for all your credit cards.

Use these tips to build your credit report and get access to funds to ensure your business has enough capital to say ahead. In addition, building your credit will allow you to leverage and add more cars to your fleet.

Applying for Credit Cards

In this section, you'll learn how to get credit cards with only inquiry per bureau. Use the methods below in the order listed below. Feel free to do your research to determine which bank or credit union pulls from the credit bureaus.

Application Inquiry #1- Alliant, who pulls from Equifax,

Application Inquiry #2- Barclays pulls from TransUnion,

Application Inquiry #3- Bank of America pulls from Equifax (includes two applications)

Application Inquiry #4- Capital One

Alliant Credit Union is not a bank but a credit union. They have a membership-only credit union, and you gain access to them by donating at least $5 to a charity of their choosing, and they will allow you to join.

Once you do that and you have a good credit report, you can access tens and thousands of dollars from the bank.

Barclays is another option. They have a unique site where you can apply for their aviator card. Interestingly, they have perks attached to their credits. After applying for Barclays and being approved, you work your way to get that sign-on bonus. Once you reach the sign-on bonus, you can bring a companion for your next flight for free.

The next step is registering for Bank of America. You're going to apply for two cards: Bank of America Business Advantage Card and the Bank of America Advantage Cash Card. These will be two inquiries.

Once you've done that, you're going to apply for three Capital One venture cards. You'll apply to all of them simultaneously; an important factor to note is that Capital One pulls from every bureau, so that will be one hard pull from each of the cards.

Now that you have applied for these seven cards, you only have a few pulls from each credit bureau. Once approved, make your payments on time for six months. After you have made all of your payments on time, request a credit line increase every six months to eight months. This is how you can access a lot of money in a short time using your good credit.

If you follow this correctly, you can build a good credit report within 60 to 90 days; this is faster when done correctly, and you will have access to business capital. I used these techniques to grow my business exponentially.

> Visit Crfortunes.com to get access to my course that will teach you more secrets on car rentals. Use code "Noelle 40" for huge savings!

CAR RENTAL FORTUNES

BUILD A PROFIT MACHINE
USING RENTAL CARS

609 Dispute Letter

WHAT'S NEEDED

- Credit report with the account in question circled and/or highlighted
- Birth certificate
- Social Security card
- Passport (if you have one) – the page showing your photo and the number
- Driver's license or state-issued identification card
- Tax document that shows your SSN
- Either a rental agreement or mortgage contract with your name and address
- Utility bills with your name and address

MAKE A COPY FOR EACH BUREAU YOU WILL BE SENDING LETTERS TO

600 N Thacker Ave
Kissimmee, FL 34741

Phone: 888.479.4542
support@noellerandall.com
NOELLERANDALL.COM

CAR RENTAL FORTUNES

BUILD A PROFIT MACHINE
USING RENTAL CARS

LETTER FORMAT

Your Name
123 Main Street
San Francisco, CA 94109
(111) 222-3333

12/31/2019

Subject: Fair Credit Reporting Act, Section 609

Dear Credit Reporting Agency (Experian, TransUnion, or Equifax),

I am exercising my right under the Fair Credit Reporting Act, Section 609, to request information regarding an item that is listed on my consumer credit report: ABC Collection Agency, account number 0123456789.

As per Section 609, I am entitled to see the source of the information, which is the original contract that contains my signature.

My identifying information is as follows:

Date of Birth: 01/21/1989
SSN: 123-45-6789

[If you have a lawyer, state that you have legal representation and provide that person's contact information]

As proof of my identity, I have included copies of my birth certificate, Social Security card, passport, driver's license, W-2, rental agreement, and a cellphone bill. I have also included a copy of my credit report with the account I am requesting to have verified circled and highlighted.

If you are unable to verify the account with the original contract, the information should be removed from my credit report within 30 days.

Sincerely,

[Signature]

You will need to assemble three separate packets and send one to each of the credit reporting agencies (assuming all are reporting the same account). Include a copy of your letter and copies of the supporting documents. Keep one set of the letter and documents for your own records.

600 N Thacker Ave
Kissimmee, FL 34741

Phone: 888.479.4542
support@noellerandall.com
NOELLERANDALL.COM

CAR RENTAL FORTUNES

BUILD A PROFIT MACHINE
USING RENTAL CARS

SEND LETTERS TO

Experian
P.O. Box 4500
Allen, TX 75013

TransUnion Consumer Solutions
P.O. Box 2000
Chester, PA 19016-2000

Equifax
P.O. Box 740241
Atlanta, GA 30374-0241

Do NOT just drop off your letters into any corner mailbox — these are very important letters, and you'll want to be sure they arrive and not get lost in transit. Go to the post office and send them via certified mail, return receipt requested. Sending them from the U.S. Post Office this way will cost under $8 per letter, so it's a pretty cheap investment.

600 N Thacker Ave

Kissimmee, FL 34741

Phone: 888.479.4542
support@noellerandall.com
NOELLERANDALL.COM

CHAPTER XI

BUILD A SUCCESSFUL BUSINESS

"*Everyone Wants to Live on Top of the Mountain, But All the Happiness and Growth Occurs While You're Climbing It.*"
Andy Rooney

Congratulations Millionaire,

You have reached the end of this book, and I want to let you know that you have made an excellent decision to create your path to becoming wealthy. I applaud you for taking this time to grow as a person and explore a new path to a better life. I remember when I was in your shoes, I felt lost with no sense of direction or knowledge of how I would arrive at where I am today. But I did it, and so can you!

Before we close out this book, I want to leave you with some last-minute Turo secrets to help you build your successful business. By now, you have learned the ins and outs of starting your Turo business. You know how Turo works, what types of cars you should list on the platform, and what mistakes you should avoid. I want to take it further and teach you how to be a Turo All-Star!

Tip #1- Conduct a Complete Detailed Inspection of Your Car

It is vital that you do this before you list your car on Turo. The reason for this is that you want proof that your car is in tip-top shape to avoid any denied claims in the future. I recommend you have the diagnostics performed at the beginning of every quarter. By taking this extra step, you will have reports with proof that your car was fully functioning at the time of listing and there aren't any recalls on the vehicle.

This is a great tip to ensure your car is always covered, and the documentation will make your reimbursement process smoother if anything happens to your car. It would be best if you did this in conjunction with taking detailed pictures of your car. If anything ever happens, for example, your engine goes out, or someone damages your car and its inoperable, you want to have proof that it was in working condition before they rented your car.

Do not skip this step. I have spoken to other hosts on the platform who did not take this extra precaution, and they suffered financial loss due to their vehicles being inoperable. I highly recommend that you do this.

Tip 2- Keep Your Car Warranties in One Place

Keep a folder full of all of your car warranties. I know this may seem simple, but it is also simple enough to be overlooked. It is very important to always keep track of all the warranties for your car. This includes your tires, brakes, transmission and oil changes. You want to keep a complete list of all the warranties because if anything happens to your car, you want to make sure you are not the one who has to pay for all the work to fix the car. I do this with my entire fleet of cars. Also, it is essential to know what your warranties cover and when they end because you may want to extend these warranties.

Tip 3- Automate Your Process

To grow in business, you must automate your business. When you first begin, you will have your hands in everything, but as you grow, you will want to simplify and automate your process.

Here is just one example- create response templates you can copy and paste for:

Reply Messages- Instead of typing out each message and responding to a guest, complete a template you can copy and paste.

Guest Bookings- *Once your guest books your car, 24 hours before their trip and at the end of their trip,* have your review request template ready.

Taking the time to create messages you can copy and paste will make responding to your guests easier. You can also train your staff to do this as well, ensuring a proper representation of your company. Having an automated business is an easy way to take things off your plate so that you can focus on income-producing activities to grow your business.

Tip 4- Create Two Business Accounts

This is a great tip that is not just for Turo but for any of the businesses you operate. Having two business accounts will help you to scale, and it is a way to get funding so that you can acquire more cars and take care of all your expenses. Let me break this down a bit further.

Account #1

This is the account you will use to collect your business income. This account will be a funnel for all your money, and you can use this account to show banks and lenders your income sources and amounts.

Account #2

This second account is for your expenses. You will use account # 1 to funnel money into account # 2. With the separation of the accounts, you can budget and manage your money. You will know exactly how much money you spend monthly spend.

Doing will help you track your expenses to ensure everything is paid from a single account. Since it is not linked to another account, there will not be any unknown charges or drafts that have not been authorized. In addition, account number #1 will be utilized to get more money, and you have a track record and bank statements to show how much money you make.

Tip 5- Find (Budget-Friendly) Ways to Make Your Car Stand Out

To my car enthusiasts, I have to burst your bubble and tell you that customizing your car to make it stand out is not the most important thing to Turo. However, although Turo is not impressed, it can help you stand out to potential guests. If you decide to add additional features, try not to go overboard. Before purchasing expensive rims, putting decals on your car, or paying for a new paint job, consider a budget-friendly option first.

There are easy and effective ways to stand out without breaking the bank.

Window Tint

Window tints can make your car stand out, and budget-friendly options are available.

Car Rims

I have rims on all my cars; however, I like the stock rims. I do not go overboard trying to change them. I've done the research and noticed that simplicity stands out.

Car Wraps

Wrapping your car will offer a color change to the car without breaking the bank, and it protects the car's natural finish, which will help with the resale value of your car.

Let me reiterate that customizing your vehicle is not necessary to stand out because many cars on the platform are stock. What helps you stand out is your description of your car, photos, and pricing. That is the most crucial part of doing well on this platform.

I hope you have found the information in this book to be beneficial. You have been armed with the knowledge, tips, and tricks I use, that will help you to succeed in this industry. Be diligent in your quest for success, and you will live the life of your dreams.

To Your Success!

Visit Crfortunes.com to get access to my course that will teach you more secrets on car rentals. Use code "Noelle 40" for huge savings!

About Noelle

Noelle Randall, MPS, MBA, is an Entrepreneur, Real Estate Investor, Author, Speaker, and all-around leader who is here to help!

Noelle is all about growth. She has been a thriving entrepreneur for over 20 years and is a successful businesswoman, best-selling author, and real-estate entrepreneur. Her diverse business experience has been instrumental in her personal success as well as the success of countless people across the country.

She teaches real estate investing to thousands of people from varying backgrounds who are ready to transform their financial status. Noelle is a full-time real estate investor and founder of the Noelle Randall Coaching Program. She provides training, workshops and hosts events to teach how to start from scratch and build a successful real estate investing business.

As CEO of Noelle Randall Coaching, Noelle offers entrepreneurs business opportunities, allowing hundreds to create wealth and financial independence through her mentorship. She has also created the opportunity to become an owner of properties across the country and obtain passive income for investors of her crowdfunded company Nuurez Inc." Additionally, Noelle is the Executive Director of the Marley Simms Foundation, a public, non-profit organization dedicated to promoting children's literacy. Its mission is to advance the diversity of thought in children by providing access and awareness to books from diverse authors and discussing diverse topics.

Noelle is the founder and president of FDR Horizon Enterprises, a private real estate equity firm, and brand manager. The company owns a diverse portfolio of real estate and has created numerous profitable and top-selling brands, including her signature product, Tea More Skinny (TeaMoreSkinny.com). In addition, Noelle is the co-founder of Bella J Hair (BellaJHair.com), the premier virgin hair extension brand and international hair and wig distributor.

In addition to being a tenacious entrepreneur and businesswoman, Noelle considers herself a perpetual student, always learning and growing. Noelle proudly boasts two advanced degrees. She earned her Bachelor's Degree from the University of Connecticut in Urban Planning. She has a Master's Degree in Economic Development from Penn State, and most recently, she earned a Master's in Business Administration (MBA) from Baylor University.

Noelle is also the proud mother of seven children, whom she credits as her inspiration for every endeavor.

Connect with Noelle

Noelle Randall, MPS, MBA, is an engaging, transparent, and powerful speaker for audiences wishing to learn real estate and live the lives they have always wanted.

Noelle is always willing to help and teach new methods and techniques to those who might actually need them. She incorporates her teachings into her life. She does not hesitate to educate people about the secrets to becoming a millionaire in real estate. Her goal is to help and make more people become millionaires like herself.

Noelle is devoted to helping more people, and she can be sought through her website www.noellerandall.com or her social media accounts:

facebook.com/noellerandallcoaching
https://twitter.com/noelle_randall
https://www.instagram.com/noellerandallcoaching/
https://youtube.com/c/noellerandall1
Email: contact@noellerandall.com

Made in the USA
Columbia, SC
08 December 2023